50 Classic Pizza Recipes

By: Kelly Johnson

Table of Contents

- Margherita Pizza
- Pepperoni Pizza
- Hawaiian Pizza
- Meat Lovers Pizza
- Veggie Supreme Pizza
- Margherita with Pesto
- Four Cheese Pizza
- BBQ Chicken Pizza
- White Pizza with Ricotta
- Mediterranean Pizza
- Buffalo Chicken Pizza
- Sausage and Peppers Pizza
- Supreme Pizza
- Margherita with Prosciutto
- Caprese Pizza
- Mushroom and Spinach Pizza
- Garlic Parmesan Chicken Pizza
- Meatball Pizza
- Veggie and Goat Cheese Pizza
- Bacon and Egg Breakfast Pizza
- Spinach and Artichoke Pizza
- Classic Neapolitan Pizza
- Roasted Garlic and Shrimp Pizza
- Pesto Chicken Pizza
- Shrimp Scampi Pizza
- Focaccia Pizza
- BBQ Pork Pizza
- Roasted Vegetable Pizza
- Chicken Caesar Pizza
- Smoked Salmon Pizza
- Anchovy Pizza
- Classic Cheese Pizza
- Prosciutto and Arugula Pizza
- Pepperoni and Mushroom Pizza
- Italian Sausage and Onion Pizza

- Ricotta and Spinach Pizza
- Fig and Prosciutto Pizza
- Philly Cheesesteak Pizza
- Breakfast Sausage Pizza
- Pappadew Pepper and Sausage Pizza
- Cheeseburger Pizza
- Philly Cheesesteak Pizza
- Shrimp and Pesto Pizza
- Spicy Italian Sausage Pizza
- Tomato and Basil Pizza
- Mexican Taco Pizza
- Fig and Blue Cheese Pizza
- Peking Duck Pizza
- Grilled Chicken and Avocado Pizza
- Roasted Beet and Goat Cheese Pizza

Margherita Pizza

Ingredients:

- 1 pizza dough
- 1/2 cup tomato sauce
- 1 cup fresh mozzarella
- Fresh basil leaves
- Olive oil for drizzling

Instructions:

1. Preheat your oven to 475°F (245°C).
2. Roll out the pizza dough on a lightly floured surface.
3. Spread tomato sauce evenly over the dough.
4. Top with fresh mozzarella.
5. Bake for 10-12 minutes until the crust is golden.
6. Remove from the oven and garnish with fresh basil leaves. Drizzle with olive oil before serving.

Pepperoni Pizza

Ingredients:

- 1 pizza dough
- 1/2 cup tomato sauce
- 1 cup shredded mozzarella cheese
- 1/2 cup sliced pepperoni

Instructions:

1. Preheat your oven to 475°F (245°C).
2. Spread tomato sauce evenly on the pizza dough.
3. Top with mozzarella cheese and pepperoni slices.
4. Bake for 10-12 minutes until the crust is golden and the cheese is bubbly.
5. Serve hot.

Hawaiian Pizza

Ingredients:

- 1 pizza dough
- 1/2 cup tomato sauce
- 1 cup shredded mozzarella cheese
- 1/2 cup diced ham
- 1/2 cup pineapple chunks

Instructions:

1. Preheat your oven to 475°F (245°C).
2. Spread tomato sauce on the pizza dough.
3. Top with mozzarella cheese, diced ham, and pineapple chunks.
4. Bake for 10-12 minutes, until golden and bubbly.
5. Serve hot.

Meat Lovers Pizza

Ingredients:

- 1 pizza dough
- 1/2 cup tomato sauce
- 1 cup shredded mozzarella cheese
- 1/2 cup cooked sausage
- 1/2 cup cooked bacon bits
- 1/2 cup sliced pepperoni
- 1/2 cup cooked ground beef

Instructions:

1. Preheat your oven to 475°F (245°C).
2. Spread tomato sauce on the dough.
3. Top with mozzarella cheese and meat toppings: sausage, bacon, pepperoni, and ground beef.
4. Bake for 10-12 minutes, until the crust is golden and cheese is melted.
5. Serve hot.

Veggie Supreme Pizza

Ingredients:

- 1 pizza dough
- 1/2 cup tomato sauce
- 1 cup shredded mozzarella cheese
- 1/4 cup sliced bell peppers
- 1/4 cup sliced mushrooms
- 1/4 cup red onion slices
- 1/4 cup black olives
- Fresh spinach leaves

Instructions:

1. Preheat your oven to 475°F (245°C).
2. Spread tomato sauce on the pizza dough.
3. Top with mozzarella cheese and the sliced vegetables.
4. Bake for 10-12 minutes until the crust is golden and the cheese is bubbly.
5. Garnish with fresh spinach leaves before serving.

Margherita with Pesto

Ingredients:

- 1 pizza dough
- 1/2 cup tomato sauce
- 1/2 cup pesto sauce
- 1 cup fresh mozzarella
- Fresh basil leaves

Instructions:

1. Preheat your oven to 475°F (245°C).
2. Spread a thin layer of tomato sauce and pesto sauce over the dough.
3. Top with fresh mozzarella.
4. Bake for 10-12 minutes, until golden.
5. Garnish with fresh basil leaves before serving.

Four Cheese Pizza

Ingredients:

- 1 pizza dough
- 1/2 cup tomato sauce
- 1/4 cup shredded mozzarella cheese
- 1/4 cup grated Parmesan cheese
- 1/4 cup crumbled blue cheese
- 1/4 cup ricotta cheese

Instructions:

1. Preheat your oven to 475°F (245°C).
2. Spread tomato sauce on the pizza dough.
3. Top with all four cheeses: mozzarella, Parmesan, blue cheese, and ricotta.
4. Bake for 10-12 minutes until the cheese is melted and the crust is golden.
5. Serve hot.

BBQ Chicken Pizza

Ingredients:

- 1 pizza dough
- 1/2 cup BBQ sauce
- 1 cup shredded mozzarella cheese
- 1/2 cup cooked chicken breast, shredded
- 1/4 cup red onion slices
- Fresh cilantro for garnish

Instructions:

1. Preheat your oven to 475°F (245°C).
2. Spread BBQ sauce over the dough.
3. Top with mozzarella cheese, shredded chicken, and red onion slices.
4. Bake for 10-12 minutes until golden.
5. Garnish with fresh cilantro before serving.

White Pizza with Ricotta

Ingredients:

- 1 pizza dough
- 1/2 cup ricotta cheese
- 1 cup shredded mozzarella cheese
- 2 tablespoons olive oil
- 2 cloves garlic, minced
- Fresh thyme or rosemary for garnish (optional)
- Salt and pepper, to taste

Instructions:

1. Preheat your oven to 475°F (245°C).
2. Roll out the pizza dough on a floured surface.
3. Spread ricotta cheese evenly over the dough.
4. Sprinkle shredded mozzarella on top of the ricotta.
5. Drizzle with olive oil and sprinkle minced garlic, salt, and pepper over the pizza.
6. Bake for 10-12 minutes until the crust is golden and cheese is melted.
7. Garnish with fresh thyme or rosemary, if desired, and serve.

Mediterranean Pizza

Ingredients:

- 1 pizza dough
- 1/2 cup tomato sauce
- 1 cup shredded mozzarella cheese
- 1/4 cup kalamata olives, sliced
- 1/4 cup sun-dried tomatoes, chopped
- 1/4 cup red onion, thinly sliced
- 1/4 cup feta cheese, crumbled
- Fresh oregano or basil for garnish

Instructions:

1. Preheat your oven to 475°F (245°C).
2. Spread tomato sauce over the pizza dough.
3. Top with mozzarella cheese, olives, sun-dried tomatoes, red onion, and crumbled feta.
4. Bake for 10-12 minutes, until the crust is golden and cheese is melted.
5. Garnish with fresh oregano or basil before serving.

Buffalo Chicken Pizza

Ingredients:

- 1 pizza dough
- 1/2 cup buffalo sauce
- 1 cup shredded mozzarella cheese
- 1 cup cooked chicken breast, shredded
- 1/4 cup red onion, thinly sliced
- 1/4 cup blue cheese crumbles
- Fresh cilantro for garnish

Instructions:

1. Preheat your oven to 475°F (245°C).
2. Spread buffalo sauce evenly over the pizza dough.
3. Top with mozzarella cheese, shredded chicken, red onion, and blue cheese crumbles.
4. Bake for 10-12 minutes until golden and bubbly.
5. Garnish with fresh cilantro and serve.

Sausage and Peppers Pizza

Ingredients:

- 1 pizza dough
- 1/2 cup tomato sauce
- 1 cup shredded mozzarella cheese
- 1/2 cup cooked sausage, crumbled
- 1/4 cup bell peppers, sliced
- 1/4 cup red onion, sliced
- Olive oil for drizzling

Instructions:

1. Preheat your oven to 475°F (245°C).
2. Spread tomato sauce over the pizza dough.
3. Top with mozzarella cheese, cooked sausage, bell peppers, and red onion.
4. Drizzle lightly with olive oil.
5. Bake for 10-12 minutes, until the crust is golden and cheese is bubbly.
6. Serve hot.

Supreme Pizza

Ingredients:

- 1 pizza dough
- 1/2 cup tomato sauce
- 1 cup shredded mozzarella cheese
- 1/4 cup pepperoni slices
- 1/4 cup bell peppers, sliced
- 1/4 cup mushrooms, sliced
- 1/4 cup black olives, sliced
- 1/4 cup sausage, crumbled

Instructions:

1. Preheat your oven to 475°F (245°C).
2. Spread tomato sauce over the pizza dough.
3. Top with mozzarella cheese and all the toppings: pepperoni, bell peppers, mushrooms, olives, and sausage.
4. Bake for 10-12 minutes, until the crust is golden and cheese is melted.
5. Serve hot.

Margherita with Prosciutto

Ingredients:

- 1 pizza dough
- 1/2 cup tomato sauce
- 1 cup fresh mozzarella
- 1/4 cup prosciutto, thinly sliced
- Fresh basil leaves
- Olive oil for drizzling

Instructions:

1. Preheat your oven to 475°F (245°C).
2. Spread tomato sauce over the pizza dough.
3. Top with mozzarella cheese and bake for 10-12 minutes until golden.
4. Once out of the oven, arrange prosciutto on top and garnish with fresh basil.
5. Drizzle with olive oil before serving.

Caprese Pizza

Ingredients:

- 1 pizza dough
- 1/2 cup tomato sauce
- 1 cup fresh mozzarella
- 1/2 cup fresh tomatoes, sliced
- Fresh basil leaves
- Olive oil for drizzling
- Balsamic glaze for drizzling

Instructions:

1. Preheat your oven to 475°F (245°C).
2. Spread tomato sauce over the pizza dough.
3. Top with fresh mozzarella and sliced tomatoes.
4. Bake for 10-12 minutes until the crust is golden and cheese is melted.
5. Garnish with fresh basil and drizzle with olive oil and balsamic glaze before serving.

Mushroom and Spinach Pizza

Ingredients:

- 1 pizza dough
- 1/2 cup tomato sauce
- 1 cup shredded mozzarella cheese
- 1/2 cup mushrooms, sliced
- 1/4 cup spinach leaves
- 2 cloves garlic, minced
- Olive oil for drizzling

Instructions:

1. Preheat your oven to 475°F (245°C).
2. Spread tomato sauce over the pizza dough.
3. Top with mozzarella cheese, mushrooms, spinach, and garlic.
4. Drizzle lightly with olive oil.
5. Bake for 10-12 minutes until the crust is golden and cheese is melted.
6. Serve hot.

Garlic Parmesan Chicken Pizza

Ingredients:

- 1 pizza dough
- 1/2 cup Alfredo sauce
- 1 cup cooked chicken breast, shredded
- 1/2 cup shredded mozzarella cheese
- 1/4 cup grated Parmesan cheese
- 2 cloves garlic, minced
- Fresh parsley for garnish (optional)

Instructions:

1. Preheat your oven to 475°F (245°C).
2. Spread Alfredo sauce over the pizza dough.
3. Top with shredded chicken, mozzarella, Parmesan, and minced garlic.
4. Bake for 10-12 minutes until the crust is golden and the cheese is melted.
5. Garnish with fresh parsley and serve.

Meatball Pizza

Ingredients:

- 1 pizza dough
- 1/2 cup tomato sauce
- 1 cup shredded mozzarella cheese
- 6-8 cooked meatballs, sliced
- 1/4 cup red onion, thinly sliced
- 1 tablespoon dried oregano
- Fresh basil for garnish

Instructions:

1. Preheat your oven to 475°F (245°C).
2. Spread tomato sauce evenly over the pizza dough.
3. Top with mozzarella cheese, sliced meatballs, red onion, and oregano.
4. Bake for 10-12 minutes until the cheese is melted and bubbly.
5. Garnish with fresh basil and serve.

Veggie and Goat Cheese Pizza

Ingredients:

- 1 pizza dough
- 1/2 cup tomato sauce
- 1 cup shredded mozzarella cheese
- 1/4 cup goat cheese, crumbled
- 1/4 cup red bell pepper, sliced
- 1/4 cup mushrooms, sliced
- 1/4 cup spinach leaves
- 1/4 cup red onion, thinly sliced
- Olive oil for drizzling

Instructions:

1. Preheat your oven to 475°F (245°C).
2. Spread tomato sauce over the pizza dough.
3. Top with mozzarella cheese, goat cheese, bell pepper, mushrooms, spinach, and red onion.
4. Drizzle with olive oil.
5. Bake for 10-12 minutes until the crust is golden and the cheese is melted.
6. Serve hot.

Bacon and Egg Breakfast Pizza

Ingredients:

- 1 pizza dough
- 1/2 cup Alfredo sauce
- 1 cup shredded mozzarella cheese
- 4 slices cooked bacon, crumbled
- 2 eggs
- 1/4 cup green onions, sliced
- Salt and pepper, to taste

Instructions:

1. Preheat your oven to 475°F (245°C).
2. Spread Alfredo sauce over the pizza dough.
3. Sprinkle mozzarella cheese, bacon, and green onions on top.
4. Crack eggs directly onto the pizza (one egg per pizza or two for extra richness).
5. Bake for 10-12 minutes until the egg whites are set and the crust is golden.
6. Season with salt and pepper, and serve hot.

Spinach and Artichoke Pizza

Ingredients:

- 1 pizza dough
- 1/2 cup Alfredo sauce
- 1 cup shredded mozzarella cheese
- 1/2 cup spinach, wilted
- 1/4 cup artichoke hearts, chopped
- 2 cloves garlic, minced
- 1/4 cup grated Parmesan cheese

Instructions:

1. Preheat your oven to 475°F (245°C).
2. Spread Alfredo sauce over the pizza dough.
3. Top with mozzarella cheese, spinach, artichokes, garlic, and Parmesan.
4. Bake for 10-12 minutes until the cheese is melted and the crust is golden.
5. Serve hot.

Classic Neapolitan Pizza

Ingredients:

- 1 pizza dough
- 1/2 cup tomato sauce
- 1 cup fresh mozzarella, sliced
- 1/4 cup fresh basil leaves
- Olive oil for drizzling

Instructions:

1. Preheat your oven to 475°F (245°C).
2. Spread tomato sauce over the pizza dough.
3. Top with mozzarella cheese slices.
4. Bake for 10-12 minutes until the crust is golden and the cheese is bubbly.
5. Garnish with fresh basil leaves and drizzle with olive oil.
6. Serve hot.

Roasted Garlic and Shrimp Pizza

Ingredients:

- 1 pizza dough
- 1/2 cup garlic butter sauce (or olive oil and garlic)
- 1 cup cooked shrimp, peeled and deveined
- 1 cup shredded mozzarella cheese
- 2 cloves garlic, minced
- 1/4 cup fresh parsley, chopped

Instructions:

1. Preheat your oven to 475°F (245°C).
2. Spread garlic butter sauce over the pizza dough.
3. Top with shrimp, mozzarella cheese, and minced garlic.
4. Bake for 10-12 minutes until the crust is golden and the cheese is melted.
5. Garnish with fresh parsley and serve.

Pesto Chicken Pizza

Ingredients:

- 1 pizza dough
- 1/4 cup pesto sauce
- 1 cup cooked chicken breast, shredded
- 1 cup shredded mozzarella cheese
- 1/4 cup sun-dried tomatoes, chopped
- Fresh basil for garnish

Instructions:

1. Preheat your oven to 475°F (245°C).
2. Spread pesto sauce over the pizza dough.
3. Top with shredded chicken, mozzarella cheese, and sun-dried tomatoes.
4. Bake for 10-12 minutes until the crust is golden and the cheese is melted.
5. Garnish with fresh basil and serve.

Shrimp Scampi Pizza

Ingredients:

- 1 pizza dough
- 1/2 cup garlic butter sauce (or olive oil and garlic)
- 1 cup cooked shrimp, peeled and deveined
- 1 cup shredded mozzarella cheese
- 1/4 cup Parmesan cheese, grated
- 1/4 teaspoon red pepper flakes (optional)
- 1 tablespoon fresh parsley, chopped

Instructions:

1. Preheat your oven to 475°F (245°C).
2. Spread garlic butter sauce evenly over the pizza dough.
3. Top with shrimp, mozzarella cheese, and Parmesan.
4. Sprinkle red pepper flakes (if using) over the top.
5. Bake for 10-12 minutes until the crust is golden and the cheese is melted.
6. Garnish with fresh parsley and serve hot.

Focaccia Pizza

Ingredients:

- 1 focaccia bread, sliced in half
- 1/2 cup tomato sauce or pesto sauce
- 1 cup shredded mozzarella cheese
- 1/4 cup black olives, sliced
- 1/4 cup cherry tomatoes, halved
- Fresh rosemary or basil leaves
- Olive oil for drizzling

Instructions:

1. Preheat your oven to 375°F (190°C).
2. Slice the focaccia bread in half horizontally and place on a baking sheet.
3. Spread the tomato or pesto sauce evenly over the bread.
4. Top with mozzarella, olives, cherry tomatoes, and rosemary.
5. Drizzle with olive oil.
6. Bake for 10-12 minutes until the cheese is melted and bubbly.
7. Garnish with fresh basil leaves and serve.

BBQ Pork Pizza

Ingredients:

- 1 pizza dough
- 1/4 cup BBQ sauce
- 1 cup cooked pork, shredded
- 1/2 cup red onion, thinly sliced
- 1 cup shredded mozzarella cheese
- 1/4 cup cilantro, chopped

Instructions:

1. Preheat your oven to 475°F (245°C).
2. Spread BBQ sauce evenly over the pizza dough.
3. Top with shredded pork, red onion, and mozzarella cheese.
4. Bake for 10-12 minutes until the crust is golden and the cheese is melted.
5. Garnish with fresh cilantro and serve.

Roasted Vegetable Pizza

Ingredients:

- 1 pizza dough
- 1/2 cup tomato sauce or olive tapenade
- 1/4 cup zucchini, sliced
- 1/4 cup bell pepper, sliced
- 1/4 cup eggplant, sliced
- 1/4 cup red onion, thinly sliced
- 1 cup shredded mozzarella cheese
- 1/4 cup Parmesan cheese, grated

Instructions:

1. Preheat your oven to 475°F (245°C).
2. Spread tomato sauce or olive tapenade over the pizza dough.
3. Top with roasted vegetables and mozzarella cheese.
4. Sprinkle Parmesan cheese over the top.
5. Bake for 10-12 minutes until the crust is golden and the cheese is melted.
6. Serve hot.

Chicken Caesar Pizza

Ingredients:

- 1 pizza dough
- 1/2 cup Caesar dressing
- 1 cup cooked chicken breast, shredded
- 1 cup shredded mozzarella cheese
- 1/4 cup Parmesan cheese, grated
- Romaine lettuce, shredded (for topping)
- Croutons, crushed (optional)

Instructions:

1. Preheat your oven to 475°F (245°C).
2. Spread Caesar dressing evenly over the pizza dough.
3. Top with shredded chicken, mozzarella, and Parmesan cheese.
4. Bake for 10-12 minutes until the crust is golden and the cheese is melted.
5. Remove from the oven and top with shredded lettuce and crushed croutons.
6. Serve immediately.

Smoked Salmon Pizza

Ingredients:

- 1 pizza dough
- 1/2 cup cream cheese, softened
- 1 tablespoon fresh dill, chopped
- 1/2 cup smoked salmon, thinly sliced
- 1/4 cup red onion, thinly sliced
- 1 tablespoon capers (optional)
- Fresh lemon wedges (for serving)

Instructions:

1. Preheat your oven to 475°F (245°C).
2. Spread cream cheese evenly over the pizza dough.
3. Top with smoked salmon, red onion, and capers (if using).
4. Bake for 10-12 minutes until the crust is golden.
5. Garnish with fresh dill and serve with lemon wedges.

Anchovy Pizza

Ingredients:

- 1 pizza dough
- 1/2 cup tomato sauce
- 1 cup shredded mozzarella cheese
- 1/4 cup anchovies, drained
- 1/4 cup black olives, sliced
- Fresh parsley for garnish

Instructions:

1. Preheat your oven to 475°F (245°C).
2. Spread tomato sauce evenly over the pizza dough.
3. Top with mozzarella cheese, anchovies, and black olives.
4. Bake for 10-12 minutes until the crust is golden and the cheese is melted.
5. Garnish with fresh parsley and serve.

Classic Cheese Pizza

Ingredients:

- 1 pizza dough
- 1/2 cup tomato sauce
- 1 cup shredded mozzarella cheese
- 1/4 cup grated Parmesan cheese
- Dried oregano or fresh basil leaves for garnish

Instructions:

1. Preheat your oven to 475°F (245°C).
2. Spread tomato sauce evenly over the pizza dough.
3. Top with mozzarella cheese and Parmesan cheese.
4. Sprinkle with dried oregano or fresh basil.
5. Bake for 10-12 minutes until the crust is golden and the cheese is melted.
6. Serve hot.

Prosciutto and Arugula Pizza

Ingredients:

- 1 pizza dough
- 1/2 cup tomato sauce
- 1 cup shredded mozzarella cheese
- 6-8 slices prosciutto
- 1/2 cup fresh arugula
- 1 tablespoon olive oil
- Balsamic glaze (optional)

Instructions:

1. Preheat your oven to 475°F (245°C).
2. Spread tomato sauce evenly over the pizza dough.
3. Top with mozzarella cheese and bake for 10-12 minutes until the crust is golden and the cheese is melted.
4. Once baked, remove from the oven and top with prosciutto and fresh arugula.
5. Drizzle with olive oil and balsamic glaze, if desired.
6. Serve immediately.

Pepperoni and Mushroom Pizza

Ingredients:

- 1 pizza dough
- 1/2 cup tomato sauce
- 1 cup shredded mozzarella cheese
- 1/2 cup pepperoni slices
- 1/2 cup mushrooms, sliced
- 1/4 teaspoon dried oregano

Instructions:

1. Preheat your oven to 475°F (245°C).
2. Spread tomato sauce evenly over the pizza dough.
3. Top with mozzarella cheese, pepperoni, and mushrooms.
4. Sprinkle with dried oregano.
5. Bake for 10-12 minutes until the crust is golden and the cheese is melted.
6. Serve hot.

Italian Sausage and Onion Pizza

Ingredients:

- 1 pizza dough
- 1/2 cup tomato sauce
- 1 cup shredded mozzarella cheese
- 1/2 cup Italian sausage, cooked and crumbled
- 1/2 cup red onion, thinly sliced
- 1 tablespoon olive oil

Instructions:

1. Preheat your oven to 475°F (245°C).
2. Spread tomato sauce evenly over the pizza dough.
3. Top with mozzarella cheese, cooked sausage, and red onion.
4. Drizzle with olive oil.
5. Bake for 10-12 minutes until the crust is golden and the cheese is melted.
6. Serve immediately.

Ricotta and Spinach Pizza

Ingredients:

- 1 pizza dough
- 1/2 cup ricotta cheese
- 1/2 cup mozzarella cheese, shredded
- 1/4 cup Parmesan cheese, grated
- 1/2 cup spinach, wilted
- 1 tablespoon olive oil
- 1/4 teaspoon nutmeg (optional)

Instructions:

1. Preheat your oven to 475°F (245°C).
2. Spread ricotta cheese evenly over the pizza dough.
3. Top with mozzarella and Parmesan cheese, followed by wilted spinach.
4. Drizzle with olive oil and sprinkle with nutmeg, if desired.
5. Bake for 10-12 minutes until the crust is golden and the cheese is melted.
6. Serve hot.

Fig and Prosciutto Pizza

Ingredients:

- 1 pizza dough
- 1/2 cup ricotta cheese
- 6-8 figs, sliced
- 6-8 slices prosciutto
- 1 tablespoon honey
- Fresh rosemary (optional)

Instructions:

1. Preheat your oven to 475°F (245°C).
2. Spread ricotta cheese evenly over the pizza dough.
3. Top with figs and prosciutto.
4. Bake for 10-12 minutes until the crust is golden and the cheese is melted.
5. Drizzle with honey and garnish with rosemary, if desired.
6. Serve immediately.

Philly Cheesesteak Pizza

Ingredients:

- 1 pizza dough
- 1/2 cup tomato sauce
- 1 cup shredded mozzarella cheese
- 1/2 cup cooked steak, thinly sliced
- 1/4 cup green bell pepper, sliced
- 1/4 cup onion, sliced
- 1/4 cup provolone cheese, shredded

Instructions:

1. Preheat your oven to 475°F (245°C).
2. Spread tomato sauce evenly over the pizza dough.
3. Top with mozzarella cheese, steak, bell pepper, and onion.
4. Sprinkle provolone cheese over the top.
5. Bake for 10-12 minutes until the crust is golden and the cheese is melted.
6. Serve immediately.

Breakfast Sausage Pizza

Ingredients:

- 1 pizza dough
- 1/2 cup tomato sauce or white sauce (such as Alfredo)
- 1 cup shredded mozzarella cheese
- 1/2 cup cooked breakfast sausage, crumbled
- 1/4 cup bell pepper, diced
- 2 eggs (optional)

Instructions:

1. Preheat your oven to 475°F (245°C).
2. Spread tomato or white sauce evenly over the pizza dough.
3. Top with mozzarella cheese, cooked sausage, and bell pepper.
4. Crack two eggs onto the pizza, if desired.
5. Bake for 10-12 minutes until the crust is golden and the cheese is melted.
6. Serve immediately.

Pappadew Pepper and Sausage Pizza

Ingredients:

- 1 pizza dough
- 1/2 cup tomato sauce
- 1 cup shredded mozzarella cheese
- 1/2 cup Italian sausage, cooked and crumbled
- 1/4 cup Pappadew peppers, sliced
- Fresh basil leaves for garnish

Instructions:

1. Preheat your oven to 475°F (245°C).
2. Spread tomato sauce evenly over the pizza dough.
3. Top with mozzarella cheese, cooked sausage, and Pappadew peppers.
4. Bake for 10-12 minutes until the crust is golden and the cheese is melted.
5. Garnish with fresh basil leaves and serve immediately.

Cheeseburger Pizza

Ingredients:

- 1 pizza dough
- 1/2 cup tomato sauce or mustard
- 1 cup shredded cheddar cheese
- 1/2 cup cooked ground beef, crumbled
- 1/4 cup red onion, thinly sliced
- 1/4 cup pickles, sliced
- 1 tablespoon ketchup (optional)

Instructions:

1. Preheat your oven to 475°F (245°C).
2. Spread tomato sauce or mustard evenly over the pizza dough.
3. Top with cheddar cheese, ground beef, red onion, and pickles.
4. Bake for 10-12 minutes until the crust is golden and the cheese is melted.
5. Drizzle with ketchup, if desired, and serve hot.

Philly Cheesesteak Pizza

Ingredients:

- 1 pizza dough
- 1/2 cup tomato sauce
- 1 cup shredded mozzarella cheese
- 1/2 cup cooked steak, thinly sliced
- 1/4 cup green bell pepper, sliced
- 1/4 cup onion, sliced
- 1/4 cup provolone cheese, shredded

Instructions:

1. Preheat your oven to 475°F (245°C).
2. Spread tomato sauce evenly over the pizza dough.
3. Top with mozzarella cheese, steak, bell pepper, and onion.
4. Sprinkle provolone cheese over the top.
5. Bake for 10-12 minutes until the crust is golden and the cheese is melted.
6. Serve immediately.

Shrimp and Pesto Pizza

Ingredients:

- 1 pizza dough
- 1/2 cup pesto sauce
- 1 cup shredded mozzarella cheese
- 1/2 cup shrimp, peeled and deveined
- 1 tablespoon olive oil
- 1/4 cup sun-dried tomatoes, chopped

Instructions:

1. Preheat your oven to 475°F (245°C).
2. Spread pesto sauce evenly over the pizza dough.
3. Top with mozzarella cheese, shrimp, and sun-dried tomatoes.
4. Drizzle with olive oil.
5. Bake for 10-12 minutes until the crust is golden and the cheese is melted.
6. Serve immediately.

Spicy Italian Sausage Pizza

Ingredients:

- 1 pizza dough
- 1/2 cup tomato sauce
- 1 cup shredded mozzarella cheese
- 1/2 cup spicy Italian sausage, cooked and crumbled
- 1/4 teaspoon red pepper flakes
- 1/4 cup fresh basil, chopped

Instructions:

1. Preheat your oven to 475°F (245°C).
2. Spread tomato sauce evenly over the pizza dough.
3. Top with mozzarella cheese, spicy sausage, and red pepper flakes.
4. Bake for 10-12 minutes until the crust is golden and the cheese is melted.
5. Garnish with fresh basil and serve immediately.

Tomato and Basil Pizza

Ingredients:

- 1 pizza dough
- 1/2 cup tomato sauce
- 1 cup shredded mozzarella cheese
- 1 cup fresh tomatoes, sliced
- 1/4 cup fresh basil leaves
- 1 tablespoon olive oil

Instructions:

1. Preheat your oven to 475°F (245°C).
2. Spread tomato sauce evenly over the pizza dough.
3. Top with mozzarella cheese and sliced tomatoes.
4. Bake for 10-12 minutes until the crust is golden and the cheese is melted.
5. Once baked, top with fresh basil leaves and drizzle with olive oil.
6. Serve immediately.

Mexican Taco Pizza

Ingredients:

- 1 pizza dough
- 1/2 cup refried beans
- 1 cup shredded cheddar cheese
- 1/2 cup ground beef, cooked and crumbled
- 1/4 cup red onion, diced
- 1/4 cup bell pepper, diced
- 1/4 cup salsa
- Sour cream and cilantro for topping

Instructions:

1. Preheat your oven to 475°F (245°C).
2. Spread refried beans evenly over the pizza dough.
3. Top with cheddar cheese, ground beef, red onion, and bell pepper.
4. Bake for 10-12 minutes until the crust is golden and the cheese is melted.
5. Once baked, drizzle with salsa, and top with sour cream and cilantro.
6. Serve immediately.

Fig and Blue Cheese Pizza

Ingredients:

- 1 pizza dough
- 1/2 cup ricotta or mozzarella cheese
- 1/2 cup blue cheese, crumbled
- 1/2 cup figs, sliced
- 1 tablespoon honey
- 1 tablespoon olive oil

Instructions:

1. Preheat your oven to 475°F (245°C).
2. Spread ricotta or mozzarella cheese evenly over the pizza dough.
3. Top with blue cheese and figs.
4. Drizzle with olive oil and honey.
5. Bake for 10-12 minutes until the crust is golden and the cheese is melted.
6. Serve immediately.

Peking Duck Pizza

Ingredients:

- 1 pizza dough
- 1/2 cup hoisin sauce
- 1 cup shredded mozzarella cheese
- 1/2 cup Peking duck, shredded
- 1/4 cup cucumber, julienned
- 1/4 cup green onions, sliced

Instructions:

1. Preheat your oven to 475°F (245°C).
2. Spread hoisin sauce evenly over the pizza dough.
3. Top with mozzarella cheese, Peking duck, cucumber, and green onions.
4. Bake for 10-12 minutes until the crust is golden and the cheese is melted.
5. Serve immediately.

Grilled Chicken and Avocado Pizza

Ingredients:

- 1 pizza dough
- 1/2 cup ranch or Caesar dressing
- 1 cup shredded mozzarella cheese
- 1/2 cup grilled chicken, sliced
- 1/4 cup avocado, sliced
- 1 tablespoon cilantro, chopped

Instructions:

1. Preheat your oven to 475°F (245°C).
2. Spread ranch or Caesar dressing evenly over the pizza dough.
3. Top with mozzarella cheese, grilled chicken, and avocado slices.
4. Bake for 10-12 minutes until the crust is golden and the cheese is melted.
5. Garnish with chopped cilantro and serve immediately.

Roasted Beet and Goat Cheese Pizza

Ingredients:

- 1 pizza dough
- 1/2 cup tomato sauce
- 1 cup shredded mozzarella cheese
- 1/2 cup roasted beets, sliced
- 1/4 cup goat cheese, crumbled
- 1 tablespoon balsamic glaze

Instructions:

1. Preheat your oven to 475°F (245°C).
2. Spread tomato sauce evenly over the pizza dough.
3. Top with mozzarella cheese, roasted beets, and goat cheese.
4. Bake for 10-12 minutes until the crust is golden and the cheese is melted.
5. Drizzle with balsamic glaze and serve immediately.

www.ingramcontent.com/pod-product-compliance
Lightning Source LLC
LaVergne TN
LVHW081333060526
838201LV00055B/2625